**MISSISSIPPI WILDFLOWERS**

# MISSISSIPPI WILDFLOWERS

## Lucile Parker

PELICAN PUBLISHING COMPANY
Gretna 1981

Copyright © 1981
By Lucile Parker
All rights reserved

QK
169
.P37

**Library of Congress Cataloging in Publication Data**

Parker, Lucile.
  Mississippi wildflowers.

  Bibliography: p. 30
  Includes index.
  1. Wild flowers—Mississippi—Pictorial works.
2. Fruit—Mississippi—Pictorial works. 3. Watercolor painting, American. 4. Parker, Lucile.
I. Title.
QK169.P37    582.13'09762    80–20433
ISBN 0–88289–165–0

Manufactured in the United States of America

Published by Pelican Publishing Company, Inc.
1101 Monroe Street, Gretna, Louisiana 70053

# Contents

Preface     7

The Wildflowers: Botanical Descriptions     9

Index     27

Bibliography     30

Color Plates     33

# Preface

The state of Mississippi has a wealth of natural beauty growing on its roadsides and along its streams. The purpose of this book is to portray some of the more common and spectacular of these wild flowers and fruits in pictures and words—not for the botanist, but for the interested flower-lover, who can turn the pages and readily recognize their identity without studying cumbersome key manuals. Also, it is an earnest endeavor to promote the enjoyment and preservation of our fast-vanishing plants; some of the flowers described here are very high on the list of endangered species.

Having always loved flowers, especially wildflowers, I began years ago to sketch them in pen and ink for sheer pleasure. I marveled at the mystery and ingenuity of nature, and was led to a desire to increase my knowledge of botany. Soon I found myself painting in watercolor and studying each flower—from fragile, delicate blossoms underfoot to sturdy and robust plants, flaunting their colors along roadsides. To the farmer who does not want them they are obnoxious weeds. To nature-lovers and tourists they are lovely wildflowers. To me they are miracles that God has sown in profusion along roadsides and streams, beauties we often do not see until our attention is called to them. And they are free for all—no planting, watering, or feeding required. Just look with amazement and enjoy!

With such a bounty to choose from, a difficult decision had to be made: which plants should be included in a book? Mississippi has a rich and varied selection of native flowers, not as abundant today, but still as beautiful as when they were first spotted by the early settlers. It also has a wealth of spectacular "aliens" or "escapees," plants that have been brought here from all parts of the world. They like our environment, have become naturalized, and are now part of our landscape. Though eliminating these immigrants meant leaving out some familiar favorites, I chose to include only natives, those plants indigenous to our state. Each selection has a special beauty or interest, and grows where man did not plant or cultivate it.

Each painting was done from a fresh, living specimen in watercolor and in actual size, then reduced for publication. The plant material was either found by me or brought to me by a friend with a detailed description of its location and growing conditions. I consider it noteworthy to mention that all four of the magnolia species illustrated here—and at least one more—can be found in a small area of Forrest County, Mississippi, where I reside.

Plants are classified by families; in this book scientific family names are arranged alphabetically. Dr. Clair Brown, professor emeritus of botany at Louisiana State University, has cautioned me that even expert botanists disagree on identification. This is easily understood: one source cites 920 genera and 19,000 species in the Aster family alone. Although I am not a botanist, scientific names are necessarily used here to provide the reader with pertinent information, since some species have as many as a dozen common names that vary from one county to another, while others seem to have none. Each description therefore includes one or more common names, the genus (capitalized) and species in italics, followed by the authority, often abbreviated. If a genus is followed by "spp." the plant may be any one of a number of species within the genus.

The region covered is the state of Mississippi, but because plants are more or less migratory and know no boundaries most of the flowers illustrated here are also found in all of the southern coastal states, especially Louisiana, Alabama, and Georgia. Naturally, growing conditions vary: soil acidity, moisture, drainage, light, and shade will greatly affect the sizes, colors, and blooming seasons (given by month at the end of each description) of the plants. This may result in seeming discrepancies in the text.

It is impossible to name all who have contributed to the preparation of this book. I should like to remember and express my appreciation to my family and many friends for their assistance and encouragement over the years. Many a flower-friend has driven countless miles searching for specimens; botanists have given needed assistance in identifications; others have shared their talents and time. I am deeply indebted to all—among them Marie Hull for her patience and encouragement during my early attempts to paint; Dr. Clair A. Brown; Dr. Paul Rosso of the University of Southern Mississippi; Van Rogers, John Marberry, Lake Douglas, George Seibert, Lois Drain, Eloise Dent, and Gay Collins.

Sarah Gillespie gave invaluable assistance, and I am truly grateful, not only for the time she spent in finding and identifying specimens but also for that spent in helping me put things together. A special thanks and appreciation to Mary Kathryn Godbold for her stenographic services.

Last, but not least, I want to express my sincere appreciation to Dr. Milburn Calhoun and Pelican Publishing Company, and to my editor, Frumie Selchen, for making it possible to share with others my happiness as an artist plant-lover.

# The Wildflowers: Botanical Descriptions

### Aceraceae: Maple Family

Plate 1
RED MAPLE, SWAMP MAPLE
*Acer rubrum* L.

A widely distributed medium-sized tree that lives up to its common name in all seasons. Early flowers are reddish and inconspicuous; green leaves have reddish stalks and veins; fruits are winged double keys, red in color. In autumn, leaves turn to brilliant shades of scarlet, yellow, and orange. Widely distributed in moist bottomlands and swamps. Fruits, April to May. Fall leaves, October to November.

### Alismataceae: Water-plantain Family

Plate 2
DUCK POTATO, ARROWHEAD
*Sagittaria lancifolia* L.

A robust water-loving perennial with flower stalks taller than the paddle-shaped leaves. Notice the grouping of threes in the flowers. Widely distributed in freshwater marshes, damp roadside ditches, and sluggish streams. April to October.

### Amaryllidaceae: Amaryllis Family

Plate 3
ATAMASCO LILY
*Zephyranthes atamasco* (L.) Herbert

In spite of the name and appearance of this small bulbous perennial, it is not a true lily. It grows in clumps along the roadside; the naked stems are topped with erect and solitary white flowers. In sandy pinelands and roadside ditches. March to April.

Plate 4
SPIDER-LILY
*Hymenocallis occidentalis* (Le-Conte) Kunth

A lilylike perennial with a large bulb that sends up numerous swordlike leaves. Each leafless stalk bears several exquisite white flowers easily identified by a thin, saucer-shaped membrane uniting the stamens. Below, six long, narrow lobes suggest the legs of a spider—hence the common name. Widely distributed on banks of streams, occasionally in damp roadside ditches. July to August.

### Anacardiaceae: Sumac Family

Plate 5
WING-RIB SUMAC
*Rhus copallina* L.

A tall shrub that sometimes forms dense thickets. Leaflets are in odd numbers, usually nine to thirty-three, and the leaflet stems are distinctly winged or ribbed. In late summer, clusters of smooth red seeds are formed, and leaves turn bright red to reddish purple. This species is not poisonous. In thickets, fencerows, and old fields. July to October.

### Apocynaceae: Dogbane Family

Plate 6
BLUE-STAR, SLIM POD
*Amsonia tabernaemontana* Walter

A small smooth-stemmed perennial that usually grows in clumps; it is easily identified by clusters of small light blue stars topping stems up to two feet tall. Fruits are in pairs, up to five inches long, slender and erect on stem ends—hence the common name "slim pod." In rich woods and along stream banks. April to May.

## Aquifoliaceae: Holly Family

Plate 7
AMERICAN HOLLY
*Ilex opaca* Aiton

Of the several species of American holly, this is the one commonly associated with the Christmas season. It is a medium to fairly large tree with thick, spiny evergreen leaves. Flowers are greenish white, small and inconspicuous; male and female flowers are borne on separate trees. Attractive red fruits usually persist throughout the winter. Widely distributed in mixed woods and forests. Flowers, April. Fruits, September to January.

Plate 8
YAUPON
*Ilex vomitoria* Aiton

A treelike or shrubby plant with persistent, slightly serrate leaves. Flowers are small and insignificant, but mature into abundant, shiny scarlet berries, borne in small clusters in the leaf axils. Common in swamps and wet woods; occasional on sandy roadsides. Fruits, November to January.

## Araceae: Arum Family

Plate 9
GOLDEN CLUB, BOG TORCH
*Orontium aquaticum* L.

An aquatic that grows in clumps, arising from a deeply buried rootstock. The common name "bog torch" refers to the sheath unfolding a pure white stem topped with a "torch" of tiny, thickly embedded yellow flowers. These "candles of spring" are widely distributed in shallow streams, bogs, and ditches. March to November.

Plate 10
JACK-IN-THE-PULPIT
*Arisaema triphyllum* (L.) Schott

A shy little plant, often overlooked because its green coloring blends with its surroundings. Every plant has two leaves with three to five leaflets each. "Jack" is the upper part of the clublike structure (or spadix) within the enclosure (or spathe); the hooded tube is the "pulpit." In late summer the hood withers and the spike is covered with bright scarlet berries. In wet swamps and bogs. March to April.

## Aristolochiaceae: Birthwort Family

Plate 11
HEART LEAF, WILD GINGER
*Hexastylis arifolia* (Michaux) Small

A small ground-hugging plant with oddly veined, heart-shaped leaves mottled in different shades of green. Leaves and roots have a spicy aroma when bruised, and the flowers—"little brown jugs" hidden under humus—give us still another common name, "monkey-jugs." In this species the three lobes of the flower are not reflexed. In rich woods. April to June.

## Asclepiadaceae: Milkweed Family

Plate 12
BUTTERFLY-WEED,
ORANGE MILKWEED
*Asclepias tuberosa* L.

A conspicuous, radiantly orange-colored milkweed with hairy stems and fuzzy leaves. All milkweed flowers are complex in form, usually with reflexed petals. In this species, the little horns and hoods are erect, grouped in many flat-topped clusters on the stems. The sap is not milky. On dry, sandy land, in full sun. May to August.

Plate 13
WHITE MILKWEED
*Asclepias variegata* L.

An erect perennial with solitary, unbranched stems and wavy-edged opposite leaves. The sap is milky and the stems are usually reddish, topped by rounded clusters of white waxen flowers. Each flower has a deep red column that separates the hoodlike appendages. In pinelands and mixed woods. May to June.

## Asteraceae: Aster or Sunflower Family

**Plate 14**
SOUTHERN ASTER
*Aster hemisphericus* (Alex.) Shinners

Members of this family may be recognized by a center head or mound of tiny disk flowers surrounded by showy ray flowers, which look like petals. The southern aster is a smooth-stemmed plant with rough, stiff, very narrow leaves. Its bracts are numerous, arranged in many rows, beneath flowers borne on stalks in leaf axils. Common and widespread in sandy soil and dry woods, and on roadsides. August to October.

**Plate 15**
STOKES ASTER, STOKESIA
*Stokesia laevis* (Hill) Greene

A native southern perennial that has long been a valuable addition to many gardens. It attracts attention in its wild state, where it grows in clumps, usually with purplish stems and smooth, lance-shaped leaves. Flowers vary in color from delicate lavender to rich violet; both disk and ray flowers are present. Common in pinelands and moist roadside ditches. May to September.

**Plate 16**
BITTER-WEED
*Helenium amarum* (Raf.) H. Rock

A weedy, much-branched annual with numerous narrow leaves, often forming a rounded mass of foliage above a single erect stem. The many flower heads are yellow with hemispherical disks and toothed rays. The plant has a strong odor and imparts a bitter flavor to milk when grazed by cattle. Widespread in pastures and on roadsides. May to frost.

**Plate 17**
BLACK-EYED SUSAN
*Rudbeckia hirta* L.

A familiar roadside plant with several branched stems and rough, hairy leaves. The disk is a dense mound of tiny dark purple or brown flowers, surrounded by showy, golden yellow ray flowers. Not affected by heat or drought. Common and widespread in dry pinelands and on roadsides. May to July.

**Plate 18**
BLANKET-FLOWER, GAILLARDIA
*Gaillardia aestivalis* (Walter) H. Rock

An annual or short-lived perennial that grows singly or in clumps. The large, soft center has long, threadlike chaff between the tiny flowerets, usually dark purplish in color. Ray flowers are often absent; when present they are deeply notched, sparse, and commonly yellow with dark purple blotches at the base. The illustrated specimen, with its sand-colored rays and no blotches, is unusual. Abundant in sandy soils and on beaches and roadsides. April to November.

**Plate 19**
PURPLE CONEFLOWER
*Echinacea purpurea* (L.) Moench

A perennial with thick, fleshy roots and stems up to four feet tall. Leaves are rough, almost spiny. Flower heads are solitary, with ray flowers drooping beneath a dome-shaped cluster of disk flowers, whose bracts are spiny and extend above the flowers. Occasional in woodlands and along roadsides. June to August.

**Plate 20**
DAISY FLEABANE,
ROBIN'S-PLANTAIN
*Erigeron pulchellus* Michaux

A perennial herb, the most handsome of the fleabane species. This daisylike flower is distinguished from asters by its bracts of approximately the same length surrounding the rays in a single circle, rather than in several overlapping circles of different lengths. Occasional in idle fields and on roadsides. April to July.

Plate 21
## GOLDENROD
*Solidago pinetorum* Small

Crowded yellow flower heads are borne along the upper sides of branches that curve gracefully outward and downward. Numerous and variable leaves, stems, and flowers overlap. In woodlands, old fields, and ditch banks. August to October.

Plate 22
## FLAT-TOPPED GOLDENROD
*Solidago tenuifolia* Pursh.

A perennial with smooth stems branching above the middle, each branch bearing a flat-topped cluster of yellow flower heads. Leaves are narrow and lance-shaped. Widespread in woodlands and old fields, and along roadsides. September to November.

Plate 23
## JERUSALEM ARTICHOKE
*Helianthus tuberosus* L.

A stout sunflower growing as high as ten feet, with rough, hairy stems and leaves. The common name has nothing to do with the city of Jerusalem, but refers instead to the Italian *girasole*, meaning "turning to the sun." The edible tubers or "artichokes" were enjoyed by Indians long before white men arrived here. Widespread in clearings and damp places. August to October.

Plate 24
## JOE-PYE WEED
*Eupatorium purpureum* L.

A perennial often found up to six feet high, with toothed leaves in whorls of three to five. Numerous flower heads cluster into masses of pinkish lavender puffs. When bruised or dried, leaves and stems have a vanilla fragrance. Widespread in branch bottoms and meadows, and along roadsides. July to October.

Plate 25
## MISTFLOWER, WILD AGERATUM
*Eupatorium coelestinum* L.

A branched perennial usually less than three feet tall, growing in clumps. Leaves have wrinkled surfaces with rounded margins. Tiny, velvety soft flower heads of bluish lavender are borne in flattish clusters. Common on moist roadsides, in meadows, and along stream banks. July to October.

Plate 26
## SNEEZEWEED
*Helenium autumnale* L.

A much-branched, conspicuously winged perennial. The bases of the leaves extend down the stems, giving the appearance of wings. The numerous flower heads are yellow. Common and widespread in pastures, fields, and ditches. May to frost.

Plate 27
## SUNFLOWER, PINELAND GINSENG
*Tetragonotheca helianthoides* L.

A stout sunflowerlike perennial with large yellow center disks surrounded by yellow rays, each with a narrow tube at its base. Notice the whorl of four broad green bracts under the rays. Occasional in dry, sandy woods and pinelands. April to August.

Plate 28
## NARROW-LEAVED SUNFLOWER
*Helianthus angustifolius* L.

A slender-stemmed perennial growing as high as six feet, with narrow and linear leaves. The entire plant is rough to the touch. Flower heads have dark, purple-brown disks and yellow ray flowers. Widespread in pinelands and on roadsides. August to October.

Plate 29
PURPLE THISTLE
*Cirsium virginianum* L.

A slender-stalked thistle with narrow, spiny-toothed leaves. Flower heads are lilac or rosy purple; the outer bracts bear short spines standing straight out. Occasional in woods and open places. August to October.

Plate 30
WHORLED TICKSEED
*Coreopsis major* Walter

An erect perennial growing in small clumps. The common name refers to the whorls of leaves encircling the stem at intervals. Flower heads branch from the upper stems. Ray flowers are yellow, disk flowers a deeper yellow with touches of deep red or black. Widespread in woodlands and old fields, and along roadsides. May to August.

**Bignoniaceae: Bignonia Family**

Plate 31
CROSS VINE
*Anisostichus capreolata* (L.) Bureau

A coarse and high-climbing woody vine with branching tendrils that enable it to climb on telephone poles and in trees to a height of more than fifty feet. Handsome bell-shaped flowers provide a colorful display. Pairs of leaflets form the compound leaves. Abundant in deciduous woods, on roadsides, and in weedy fields. May to November.

Plate 32
TRUMPET-CREEPER, TRUMPET VINE
*Campsis radicans* (L.) Seemann

A close relative of cross vine, trumpet-creeper trails or climbs by means of aerial roots. Leaves are compound with seven to fifteen coarsely serrate leaflets. Flowers are sometimes solid in color, sometimes mottled, in a swollen trumpetlike shape. Common on roadsides and in clearings. June to July.

**Calycanthaceae: Calycanthus Family**

Plate 33
SWEET SHRUB
*Calycanthus floridus* L.

A deciduous shrub growing up to ten feet tall, heavily leafed. Bark, leaves, and flowers are aromatic. The flowers are composed of many strap-shaped petals and sepals. The fig-shaped fruits have many glossy brown seeds reputed to be poisonous if eaten. Widespread in rich woods and along streams. April to May.

**Caprifoliaceae: Honeysuckle Family**

Plate 34
CORAL HONEYSUCKLE,
TRUMPET HONEYSUCKLE
*Lonicera sempervirens* L.

A twining woody vine with oval green leaves; the upper pairs are fused and appear to be pierced by the stems. Slender trumpet-shaped slowers cluster in several groups at the ends of new growth. Bright scarlet outside, the flowers are yellow within. Widespread in woods and along fencerows. April to November.

**Caryophyllaceae: Pink Family**

Plate 35
FIRE PINK
*Silene virginica* L.

A small perennial easily spotted because of the fiery red color of its star-shaped blossoms. Beneath the five-petaled flower is a hairy and sticky elongated tube or calyx. Slender, weak stems carry few flowers, but the bright color of small clumps makes them conspicuous. On hillsides and clay banks, and along roadsides. May to June.

### Celastraceae: Staff-tree Family

Plate 36
HEARTS A-BUSTIN' WITH LOVE,
STRAWBERRY BUSH
*Euonymus americanus* L.

An erect or sometimes sprawling shrub with small, inconspicuous greenish purple flowers. Not until late summer does this plant come into its glory; then the rough and warty crimson capsules split open, exposing bright, glossy red seeds. Suddenly the reason for the common name becomes clear. In rich woods, ravines, and swamp forests. Flowers, May to June. Fruits, September to October.

### Commelinaceae: Dayflower Family

Plate 37
SPIDERWORT
*Tradescantia* spp.

A perennial herb reaching approximately two feet in height. Blue flowers with conspicuous yellow stamens are thickly clustered above a pair of long, narrow, leaflike bracts. Stem and leaves have a whitish bloom. In wooded thickets and meadows, and along roadsides. April to June.

### Convolvulaceae: Morning-glory Family

Plate 38
DUNE MORNING-GLORY,
BEACH MORNING-GLORY
*Ipomoea stolonifera* (Cyrillo) Poir.

A smooth, trailing vine that often forms roots at the nodes. Leathery leaves are strongly lobed. Flowers are large, white, and bell-shaped, greenish yellow in the center. Common on coastal sand dunes and beaches. August to October.

Plate 39
WILD MORNING-GLORY
*Ipomoea trichocarpa* Ell.

A trailing vine with strongly lobed leaves and stems that twine over surrounding vegetation. Flowers are pink or purplish with deeply colored centers; several are grouped on terminals of stems four to six inches long. Frequent in fencerows, along roadsides, and in fields. June to October.

Plate 40
WILD-POTATO, MAN OF EARTH
*Ipomoea pandurata* (L.) Meyer

A morning-glory, closely related to the sweet potato, that produces a large underground tuber once boiled and relished by the Indians. Leaves are thin and heart-shaped; white flowers have deep red-purple throats. In old fields and on dry, open roadsides. June to September.

### Cornaceae: Dogwood Family

Plate 41
ALTERNATE LEAF DOGWOOD
*Cornus alternifolia* L.f.

A deciduous shrub or small tree, with leaves usually crowded at the end of the twig. Flowers are tiny and white, clustered terminally, with stamens radiating out like four-spoked children's jacks. Uncommon on stream banks and in woods. April to May.

Plate 42
FLOWERING DOGWOOD (Spring)
*Cornus florida* L.

A small and graceful deciduous hardwood tree with wide-spreading branches. The genus name *Cornus* means "tough wood." Its blossoms usually appear before the leaves, or with them, and what seems to be a single flower is actually a crowded cluster of match head-sized greenish flowers surrounded by four large, petallike bracts. Widely distributed in moist, rich soils, often in the shade of other hardwoods. Late March to April.

Plate 43
FLOWERING DOGWOOD (Fall)
*Cornus florida* L.

Flowering dogwood is as striking in the fall as in the spring. Leaves turn to shades from orange to deep red, adding to the beauty of the shiny red fruits, rather large ovoid berries in lustrous clusters of two to twelve. September to November.

## Cyperaceae: Sedge Family

Plate 44
WHITE-TOPPED SEDGE
*Dichromena colorata* (L.) Hitchcock

At first glance you might think this is a lily, but it is actually a sedge. What appear to be petals are actually seven or more drooping bracts, white tapering to a dark green tip. The inconspicuous flowers are hidden in clusters of small spikelets at the base of the bracts. Abundant in moist pinelands; also found in prairies and coastal marshes. April to August.

## Ebenaceae: Ebony Family

Plate 45
PERSIMMON
*Diospyros virginiana* L.

A medium-sized hardwood tree with dark bark and deciduous, dark green leaves. Its flowers are inconspicuous, but in the fall the leaves turn yellow-green with dark blotches and the limbs are laden with large, berrylike orange fruits. When green, the fruit is bitter and astringent, but when ripe (often after frost) it is edible, pulpy, and sweet. Found in open, dry sites, on roadsides, and in old fields. Flowers, May. Fruits, October to November.

## Ericaceae: Heath Family

Plate 46
CLAMMY AZALEA,
SWAMP HONEYSUCKLE
*Rhododendron viscosum* (L.) Torrey

A shrubby azalea differing from its relative *R. canescens* in blooming after the leaves are fully developed. Leaves are slightly hairy and the few-flowered clusters of white flowers are densely hairy and sticky and very fragrant. In wet swamps, bogs, and pond margins. May to June.

Plate 47
ORANGE-FLOWERED AZALEA
*Rhododendron austrinum* (Small) Mill.

A large deciduous shrub with flowers that usually open at the same time as the leaf buds. Several flowers radiate to form a cluster of tubular blossoms flaring into five lobes or petals. Colors are variable, ranging from shades of orange and yellow to some reddish tints. In moist pinelands and along wooded streams. Abundant in localized areas in extreme southern Mississippi counties. March to April.

Plate 48
SUMMER AZALEA, SWAMP AZALEA
*Rhododendron serrulatum* (Small) Mill.

A large deciduous shrub, closely related to *R. viscosum*, but with a habit of blooming even later, long after leaves have formed. Flowers are sparsely arranged in clusters, with rather sticky and hairy tubes, spicily fragrant. In wet swamps, bogs, and pond margins. June to July.

Plate 49
WILD AZALEA,
PINK HONEYSUCKLE
*Rhododendron canescens* (Michaux) Sweet

A loosely branched deciduous shrub up to six feet tall, with small oval leaves faintly hairy above and below. Fragrant flowers are in compact clusters, opening before and sometimes with the leaves. The deep pink tube of each flower flares into five lobes or petals and is quite hairy and sticky. Widely distributed in moist pinelands and along wooded streams. March to April.

### Plate 50
### FETTERBUSH
*Leucothoe axillaris* (Lam.) D. Don

An evergreen shrub with stiff and leathery leaves. Tiny white urn-shaped flowers cluster where leaves join the stem. The illustrated specimen shows the reddish new leaves, last year's emptied seed pods, and current blossoms. In swamps and sandy stream bottoms in pinelands. March to April.

### Plate 51
### MOUNTAIN LAUREL
*Kalmia latifolia* L.

A large shrub or small tree with clusters of deep pink to white flowers when in full bloom. Individually, the deep pink buds resemble perfect little cake-frosting rosebuds. They open to intricately formed shallow cups, with anthers fitting into pockets outlined in purple. Common along streams in pinelands. April to May.

## Euphorbiaceae: Spurge Family

### Plate 52
### WILD POINSETTIA, PAINTED-LEAF
*Euphorbia heterophylla* L.

A close relative to the cultivated poinsettia, this wild cousin is a small, much-branched perennial. Both stems and leaves contain a milky latex that flows freely when the plant is cut. Flowers are clustered in the center with leaves immediately beneath, strongly marked with red and orange. In damp, sandy soil and waste places, and on wooded slopes. July to November.

## Fabaceae: Legume Family

### Plate 53
### CHEROKEE BEAN, MAMOU
*Erythrina herbacea* L.

An erect, showy plant with tender stems up to five feet tall. Leaves are compound with three leaflets; the stem has a few small prickles. Deep red flowers mature into strongly curved and twisted bean pods, which split open, exposing coral red seeds that keep their color and remain in the pods indefinitely. Widely distributed in open sandy woods and clearings, and in roadside ditches. Flowers, May to July. Fruits, September to November.

### Plate 54
### GOAT'S RUE
*Tephrosia virginiana* (L.) Persoon

Growing in clumps to about thirty inches in height, this perennial is covered with silvery hairs and numerous paired leaflets. Flowers are densely clustered at the tips of stems, pea-shaped and bicolored, cream and pink. Widespread in sandy soil and dry open woods, and along roadsides. May to June.

### Plate 55
### BLACK LOCUST
*Robinia pseudo-acacia* L.

A small tree in the South, becoming larger further north. Leaves are deciduous and featherlike, often armed at the base with sharp, spinelike stipules or thorns. Fragrant pea-shaped white flowers form a drooping cluster up to six inches long. Common along roadsides and in thickets. April to May.

### Plate 56
### LADY LUPINE
*Lupinus villosus* Willd.

A showy perennial with clusters of hairy gray-green leaves at the base of erect flowering stalks. Many pea-shaped blossoms—pale lavender in color with a deep purple spot in the center of the upper (standard) petal—are borne on the stems. Fruit is a flattish pea pod. In dry pinelands, along roadsides, and on disturbed sites. March to April.

Plate 57
PARTRIDGE PEA
*Cassia fasciculata* Michaux

A slender annual herb, sometimes branched, with many small leaflets that are slightly sensitive to the touch. Flowers are borne just above the axils of the leaves, two or three of which usually have a purple spot at the base. Stamens have yellow and purple anthers. Flowers open in the morning and wilt in the afternoon. Common in old fields, along roadsides, and in disturbed areas. June to September.

Plate 58
REDBUD
*Cercis canadensis* L.

A small tree, especially noticeable in early spring before the heart-shaped leaves appear. Myriads of pea-shaped, magenta-colored blossoms appear on branches and twigs. Fruit is a flat, many-seeded pod, turning from green to bronze to brown. Widely distributed in pinelands. Early February into March.

## Gentianaceae: Gentian Family
Plate 59
ROSE-GENTIAN
*Sabatia brachiata* Ell.

A slender annual, much-branched at the top, often reaching a height of three feet. Ovate leaves partly clasp the stem. Flowers are loosely clustered on opposite stems, each with five bright pink petals backed by five long and pointed sepals. Widespread in sandhills and along roadsides. May to August.

## Hamamelidaceae: Witch-hazel Family
Plate 60
SWEET-GUM
*Liquidambar styraciflua* L.

A tall, straight tree with thick twigs bearing corky ridges. Star-shaped leaves differ from the maple in growing alternately on the twigs. The illustrated specimen shows the brilliant fall coloring of the leaves. Common in low, moist places. October to November.

## Hippocastanaceae: Buckeye Family
Plate 61
RED BUCKEYE
*Aesculus pavia* L.

A large shrub or small tree with compound leaves; five to seven leaflets emerge from the same point on a stout stem, which is about as long as the leaflets. Terminal flower clusters are erect, with numerous dark red tubular flowers. Common along streams in hilly areas, and along roadsides. March to May.

## Illiciaceae: Illicium Family
Plate 62
STAR-ANISE, STAR-BUSH
*Illicium floridanum* Ell.

An evergreen shrub with fleshy and thick leaves that have a strong, aniselike odor when crushed. Flowers have many narrow, dark crimson petals radiating around two or more cycles of stamens. Fruit is fleshy and light green when young, with flat radiating pistils fused to form a starlike circle. In low swamps and along streams. March to May.

## Iridaceae: Iris Family
Plate 63
CRESTED DWARF IRIS
*Iris cristata* Aiton

A dwarf iris with bladelike leaves sheathing the stalk. Flowers are purplish or bluish, with three petals curving slightly upward. Three sepals curve downward, each bearing three parallel lines surrounded by white, bordered in deep blue or purple—the crest! Rarely found in low swamplands, and along streams and damp roadsides. March to April.

Plate 64
RED IRIS, COPPER-COLORED IRIS
*Iris fulva* Ker

This iris was first collected near New Orleans in 1811. Flowers are reddish in color, ranging from copper to orange, and occasionally yellow. Falls (sepals) are larger than standards (petals). Widely distributed in wet sites, fresh marshes, streams, and ponds. March to May.

Plate 65
SOUTHERN BLUE FLAG
*Iris virginica* L.

This iris usually has lavender flowers, although some are blue, and some others white. The sepals (falls) are short, with unusually long claws, giving the flowers a graceful appearance. The falls have a distinctive yellow signal patch, with conspicuous dark veins. Widespread in marshes, stream banks, and damp sites. March to April.

Plate 66
ZIG-ZAG-STEMMED IRIS
*Iris brevicaulis* Raf.

A perennial with a distinctively zig-zag stem seldom more than two feet high. Flowers emerge from bracts in the angles of stems. Deep blue or purple, the sepals (falls) are longer than the erect standards (petals). Each fall is oval-shaped, with white rays enclosing a yellow signal patch. Common in wet sites, fresh marshes, streams, and ponds. March to April.

## Lamiaceae: Mint Family

Plate 67
RED BASIL
*Satureja coccineum* (Nutt.) Kuntze

A low shrub with numerous small and opposite leaves. Flowers are solitary—a vivid scarlet that brightens dunes and sandy shores of the outer Coastal Plain throughout the year.

Plate 68
HORSEMINT
*Monarda punctata* L.

A perennial up to three feet tall with several flowers spherically clustered around the upper stem. Pointed purplish bracts surround inconspicuous pale yellow flowers with deep purple spots. Infrequently found in open mixed woods. July to October.

## Lentibulariaceae: Bladderwort Family

Plate 69
YELLOW BUTTERWORT
*Pinguicula lutea* Walter

A small perennial herb probably given its common name because the leaves have a buttery or greasy feel. Leaves are in a tight, flat rosette, with edges that roll inward; this, together with the sticky surface, enables the plant to capture and hold small insects. Flowers are solitary, with a conspicuous spur on the back of each. Occasionally found in moist, sandy pinelands. February to May.

## Liliaceae: Lily Family

Plate 70
CROW POISON
*Zigadenus angustifolia* (Michaux) Swats

A perennial growing from a bulb, with long grasslike leaves, many at the base, fewer toward the top of the stems, which may grow as high as four feet. The flower stem curves slightly and is densely crowded with small, creamy white blossoms. Petals persist after maturity and become green or purplish with age. Widespread in bogs and pinelands, and on roadsides near streams. April to May.

Plate 71
SOUTHERN PINE LILY, LEOPARD LILY
*Lilium catesbaei* Walter

A bog-loving lily that is vanishing fast; when a rare colony is seen in a secluded pineland bog, it is a burst of beauty not to be forgotten. Unlike the usual lily, each stem bears one erect, upward-facing flower, light red marked with yellow and dark spots. Petals are rounded stalks at the base and taper above to long, narrow, claw-shaped tips, leaving a sense of airy grace. In wet pinelands, bogs, and swamps. August to September.

Plate 72
PURPLE TRILLIUM,
LITTLE SWEET BETSY
*Trillium cuneatum* Raf.

Trilliums differ from most flowers in the Lily family in having three green, petallike sepals contrasting with three colored petals. Leaves are net-veined and mottled. This species is the most common; it is characterized by the flower's growing from the tip of the stem at the same point as the three leaves, with no stalk of its own. Widely distributed in moist, rich, and shaded woods. March to April.

**Loganiaceae: Logania Family**

Plate 73
INDIAN PINK
*Spigelia marilandica* L.

A tender, erect perennial, solitary or in clumps, growing up to two feet tall. Leaves are opposite, lance-shaped, hugging the stems. Flowers line up in close ranks on the curved stem, opening from the bottom to the top. Each is a slender red tube with five sharp-pointed lobes that turn back to expose a yellow interior. Often found in moist woods and creek bottoms, and occasionally on roadsides. May to June.

Plate 74
YELLOW JESSAMINE
*Gelsemium sempervirens* (L.) Aiton f.

A woody, high-climbing vine that often forms dense, tangled masses by twisting and twining over plants, fences, or even bare ground. Leaves are evergreen with slender, reddish stems. Fragrant yellow flowers are trumpet-shaped with flaring lobes. Widespread in thickets, and along fencerows and roadsides. March to April.

**Magnoliaceae: Magnolia Family**

Plate 75
COWCUMBER, UMBRELLA TREE,
BIG-LEAF MAGNOLIA
*Magnolia macrophylla* Michaux

A deciduous tree readily identified by its huge light green leaves—up to three feet long—that form an umbrella beneath the blossoms. Fragrant cup-shaped flowers are large and creamy white, with wavy and unequal petals. Violet or purple blotches dot the inner three petals. Numerous stamens and pistils are arranged spirally on an elongated receptacle. This arrangement marks the magnolia as a primitive plant; it is believed to be one of the oldest flowers and the first to grow on a tree. Frequent in ravines, along small streams, in rich woods, and on roadsides. April to May.

Plate 76
CUCUMBER TREE
*Magnolia acuminata* L.

A medium-sized tree with deciduous leaves up to seven inches long. Flowers are greenish yellow, bell-shaped, with stamens and pistils arranged like those of other magnolias. The fruit is cylindrical, slightly resembling a cucumber. Occasional on low, gentle slopes and stream banks. April to May.

Plate 77
### SOUTHERN MAGNOLIA, BULL BAY
*Magnolia grandiflora* L.

A large evergreen tree with simple leathery leaves, dark green above and often rusty-haired below. The large and fragrant flowers are cup-shaped, with thick, creamy white petals. The magnolia is the state flower of Mississippi. Widely distributed in swamp forests and along small streams. April to June; occasionally blooms into fall.

Plate 78
### SWEET BAY, SWAMP BAY
*Magnolia virginiana* L.

A large, slow-growing evergreen with leaves that are green above and silvery below. The small and fragrant white flowers resemble miniature *Magnolia grandiflora* blossoms, but the petals are more curved and rounded. Common along swamp bottoms and in poorly drained pinelands. April through May.

Plate 79
### TULIP TREE, YELLOW POPLAR
*Liriodendron tulipifera* L.

Tall and straight, with distinctive square-tipped leaves and handsome flowers, this is a tree of ancient lineage. The specific name *tulipifera* is appropriate; exotic tulip-shaped flowers are greenish yellow with a large orange blotch inside the base of each petal. Stamens and pistils are numerous on a slender, conelike receptacle. Widely distributed in rich woods and piney areas, and along highways. March to April.

## Malvaceae: Mallow Family

Plate 80
### CRIMSON-EYED MALLOW, PINELAND HIBISCUS
*Hibiscus moscheutos* L.

A perennial growing as high as four feet, with hairy stems and leaves. Large funnel-shaped flowers are white with a dark maroon center; stamens and pistils form a reddish column inside. Common in moist pinelands, and along ditches and roadsides. May to September.

Plate 81
### POPPY-MALLOW, WINE CUP
*Callirhoë papaver* (Cav.) Gray

A sprawling, slender-stemmed plant with linear, deeply cleft leaves. Flowers are solitary and scattered, rose-colored and shaped somewhat like poppies. Partly opened flowers resemble little cups full of wine. In dry woods and open fields. May to June.

## Melastomataceae: Melastoma Family

Plate 82
### MEADOW BEAUTY
*Rhexia alifanus* Walter

An erect perennial with smooth stems, reaching a height of two to three feet. Leaves are soft green, pointing upward, close to the stem. Buds are numerous and sharp-pointed, while showy magenta flowers are conspicuous with large curved and golden anthers. Widespread in moist pinelands and roadside ditches. May to September.

## Nymphaeaceae: Water-lily Family

Plate 83
### WHITE WATER-LILY
*Nymphaea odorata* Aiton

A perennial aquatic with stems that root underwater and circular floating leaves, dark green above and purplish below. Flowers are fragrant, with many white petals and numerous stamens. They open only in the morning—usually for three or four days—and close in the afternoon. Occasional in ponds, sluggish streams, and ditches. June to September.

## Onagraceae: Evening-primrose Family

Plate 84
PRIMROSE, BUTTERCUP,
WINDFLOWER
*Oenothera speciosa* Nutt.

A showy little perennial often called "buttercup" in spite of pink—and sometimes white—petals. Possibly this is due to the abundance of yellow pollen on the long anthers, which readily transfers if touched. Club-shaped buds nod downward, opening into four-petaled flowers that remain open all day. Common in colonies on ditch banks and roadsides, and in idle fields. March to June.

## Orchidaceae: Orchid Family

Plate 85
BOG ORCHID, GRASS PINK
*Calopogon pulchellus* R. Br.

A slender, erect orchid growing from a single tiny bulb. Several flowers open from the bottom up on a flowering stem. Notice the lip that extends upward instead of downward. In wet open woods, bogs, and ditches. April to June.

ROSE POGONIA
*Pogonia ophioglossoides* (L.) Ker

A delicate little orchid with a solitary leaf in the middle of the stem, terminated by a single flower. Rare; when it is found it is usually in company with the bog orchid (*Calopogon*) as in Plate 85. The two flowers share the same habitat and blooming period.

Plate 86
WHITE FRINGED-ORCHID
*Habenaria blephariglottis* (Willd.) Hooker

A slender earth-growing orchid, often found to two and one half feet tall. Many miniature white orchids top the stem; each flower has a conspicuous spur up to two inches long, and a well-developed fringe on the lower lip. This is a rare species, threatened with extinction. Occasionally found in bogs and on coastal plains. August.

Plate 87
ROSEBUD ORCHID,
SPREADING POGONIA
*Cleistes divaricata* (L.) Ames

A very slender and erect orchid easily distinguished by its spidery appearance. A single leaf is attached above the middle of the stem. The flower, usually solitary, has a tubelike form with three dark sepals erect and spreading. In moist pinelands and bogs, and on coastal plains. May to July.

## Oxalidaceae: Wood-sorrel Family

Plate 88
VIOLET WOOD SORREL
*Oxalis* spp.

A perennial herb six to twelve inches high, with leaflets similar to those of common clover. Pale pink flowers with deeper colored veins close at night and open with the sun. Widespread in clearings and idle fields, and along roadsides. March to September.

## Papaveraceae: Poppy Family

Plate 89
BLOODROOT
*Sanguinaria canadensis* L.

The common name derives from the thick underground stem that yields a brilliant orange-scarlet juice once used by Indians as a pigment. When the slender bud appears in early spring, it is wrapped in a single deeply lobed leaf; the leaf rises well above the protective sheath when the flower opens. Fragile petals quickly fall. Occasional colonies on rich wooded hillsides and in ravines. March to April.

## Passifloraceae: Passion-flower Family

**Plate 90**
**MAYPOP, PASSION-FLOWER**
*Passiflora incarnata* L.

A robust vine that climbs by means of tendrils. Delicate flowers are intricately arranged, with pale green and lavender sepals and petals, mottled fringe, and elevated stamens and ovary. The fruit is a large, many-seeded green berry (maypop); it turns yellow at maturity, when it is sometimes eaten by children. In fields and along roadsides. May to September.

**Plate 91**
**YELLOW PASSION-FLOWER**
*Passiflora lutea* L.

A tender-stemmed, miniature passion-flower with small, pale yellow flowers. Leaves are thin, with three rounded lobes. Fruit is a miniature maypop, purplish black when mature. In mixed woods and thickets. June to September.

## Polemoniaceae: Phlox Family

**Plate 92**
**CAROLINA PHLOX**
*Phlox carolina* L.

A slender perennial with flowering stems occasionally growing as high as three feet. The rounded clusters of flowers are largest at the tips of the stems, with fewer flowers and longer stalks further down. Usually in small clumps, the lavender or pink blossoms make a striking display in fields and rich woods, and along roadsides. May to July.

## Polygalaceae: Milkwort Family

**Plate 93**
**ORANGE CANDY-ROOT**
*Polygala lutea* L.

One of many little plants commonly called "candy-root" because of the wintergreen aroma and flavor of their small roots. Flower heads are dense, cloverlike, and bright orange. Locally abundant in low pinelands, sandy swamps, and bogs. March to October.

**LOW CANDY-ROOT,**
**BACHELOR'S BUTTON**
*Polygala nana* (Michaux) DC.

Very similar to orange candy-root, but much smaller, with lemon yellow flower heads. Flower stems branch out from a rosette of basal leaves. Same habitat and blooming season as *P. lutea*.

## Ranunculaceae: Crowfoot Family

**Plate 94**
**EARLY BUTTERCUP**
*Ranunculus fascicularis* Muhl.

A low-growing, spreading perennial with a cluster of cylindrical tubers. The soft, downy leaves are divided several times. The flowers are borne on separate stems, standing well above the leaves, with petals conspicuously waxy and glossy. In sunny and grassy fields, and along roadsides and fencerows. March to April.

**Plate 95**
**LEATHER-FLOWER, CLEMATIS**
*Clematis crispa* L.

A sprawling vine with many-angled stems and flowers either solitary or in groups of three, on naked stalks. The nodding flower varies in color from bluish or pinkish to violet, and is composed of petallike sepals, no petals. These thick sepals spread into pointed and ruffly margins. Also pictured is a stem of *Clematis viorna*, which was found growing alongside the *C. crispa*. It has simple margins, not wavy. Along streams and in low woods, and climbing on weeds in ditches. April to June.

## Rosaceae: Rose Family

Plate 96
WILD CRAB-APPLE,
SOUTHERN CRAB-APPLE
*Malus angustifolia* (Aiton) Michaux

A small, much-branched deciduous tree with fragrant blossoms clustered three or more together. Closed buds are deep pink, opening into distinctly clawed petals of pale pink to white. The fruit is a miniature apple, depressed at each end, smooth and yellowish when ripe. The pulp is hard, sour and fragrant, very popular for making jelly. Widely distributed in old fields and along small streams and fencerows. Flowers, March to April. Fruits, August to September.

Plate 97
PARSLEY HAWTHORN
*Crataegus marshallii* Eggl.

A small tree with spiny branches and fernlike leaves that are many-lobed and serrate; the small flowers are pinkish white with numerous stamens. The leaves resemble those of parsley plants. Widely distributed in meadows and swamps, and on fencerows. April to May.

Plate 98
MAYHAW
*Crataegus opaca* Hooker and Arn.

A small tree with deciduous leaves and branches armed with long, sharp thorns. Flowers are white, appearing shortly before and with the leaves. Fruits vary from shiny green to orange to reddish, and are shaped like miniature apples. They make a delicious jelly. Widely distributed in low, wet woods, sometimes in standing water. Fruits, May to June.

Plate 99
CAROLINA ROSE, WILD ROSE
*Rosa carolina* L.

A slender little rose, seldom more than two feet high, with thorns that are slender and straight. Leaves are compound, with five to nine leaflets. Solitary flowers of pale pink have long and slender sepals and numerous pistils and stamens. One-seeded fruits are enclosed in "hips." Abundant in open woods and pinelands. May through June.

Plate 100
SOUTHERN DEWBERRY (Flower)
*Rubus trivialis* Michaux

A densely thorny shrub with trailing or arching branches, one of a large species collectively called "brambles." Stems are covered with spines and thorns. It can be distinguished from the blackberry by its solitary flowers; the blackberry has many-flowered clusters. Widespread and common along railroads and roadsides, and in old fields. March to April.

Plate 101
SOUTHERN DEWBERRY (Fruit)
*Rubus trivialis* Michaux

Dewberry flowers and fruits are borne on second-year canes. First-year canes are densely covered with bright red bristles and recurved spines. The fruits are reddish black, juicy and sweet, enjoyed by birds and humans. Late April to May.

## Rubiaceae: Madder Family

Plate 102
PARTRIDGE BERRY
*Mitchella repens* L.

A dainty little trailing evergreen vine with round and opposite leaves. Paired pink buds are united at the base, opening into waxy, white, and fragrant four-petaled flowers that are densely bearded within. Interestingly, each paired flower matures into one small red berry that shows two round eyes outlined in black. These edible fruits persist throughout the winter; they were used by Indians as a tonic. Widespread in shady mixed woods. Flowers, April to May. Fruits, September until spring.

## Sarraceniaceae: Pitcher-plant Family

Plate 103
### CRIMSON PITCHER-PLANT
*Sarracenia drummondii* Croom

One of a spectacular carnivorous plant family whose members are all perennial bog residents. They are distinguished by hollow leaves lined with downward-pointing hairs that catch and absorb unwary insects. The trumpet-shaped leaves of this species are green at the base, shading to white with a network of reddish veins in the upper portion. Deep crimson petals have fallen from the flower stalks in the illustrated specimen. In bogs and pine-cypress flatwoods near the Gulf Coast. April to May.

Plate 104
### PARROT PITCHER-PLANT
*Sarracenia psittacina* Michaux

One of the smallest of southern pitcher-plants, this plant is well-named, for the rosettes of fat little leaves resemble the beaks of parrots. A dull dark red flower nods above the short leaves. As in all pitcher-plants, the flowers appear only in spring, but the leaves retain their bright colors until fall. In sandy bogs and wet pinelands along the Mississippi coast and seventy-five miles inland. March to April.

Plate 105
### YELLOW PITCHER-PLANT
*Sarracenia flava* L.

The trumpet-shaped leaves are conspicuously veined and have hoods that arch over but do not completely cover the mouth of the pitcher. The flower hangs from a leafless stem, face toward the ground, with five yellow petals drooping from an upside-down, umbrella-shaped pistil. Abundant in sandy bogs and wet pinelands on the Mississippi Gulf Coast and as far north as Camp Shelby. March to May.

## Saxifragaceae: Saxifrage Family

Plate 106
### OAK-LEAF HYDRANGEA
*Hydrangea quercifolia* Bartr.

A straggly, laxly branched woody shrub, often reaching a height of eight feet. Leaves are coarse and woolly, deeply lobed like some oaks. Compact flower clusters contain numerous small flowers and a few much larger blossoms with four petallike sepals. These are greenish white on opening, then turn pinkish, finally a tannish brown. Widespread in moist, shady woodlands and along hilly roadsides. April to June.

Plate 107
### OAK-LEAF HYDRANGEA
*Hydrangea quercifolia* Bartr.

Although this shrub usually bears greenish white flowers (as in Plate 106), it is not unusual to find plants with large clusters of pink flowers as illustrated in Plate 107. This is an example of the variations in color that may be found in plants of the same species and under similar growing conditions. Occasionally found in the same locale, with the same blooming period, as described in Plate 106.

## Scrophulariaceae: Figwort Family

Plate 108
### PURPLE GERARDIA
*Agalinis purpurea* (L.) Pennell

An annual herb, many-branched, with tiny linear leaves. Flowers are in shades of rose or purple, trumpet-shaped with rounded lobes slightly cupped. The bottom lobe swells sharply. Just inside the throat are light purplish spots. In low, wet areas. August to October.

## Solanaceae: Nightshade Family

Plate 109
GROUND CHERRY
*Physalis angulata* L.

A member of the large Nightshade family, which includes such diverse plants as our table tomatoes, Irish potatoes, eggplants, and tobacco. This densely hairy annual has small, bell-shaped yellow flowers. The fruit is a little round green globe entirely enclosed within a papery green ten-ribbed sack that resembles a miniature Japanese lantern. Common along fencerows and roadsides, and a pest in cultivated fields. June to August.

## Styracaceae: Storax Family

Plate 110
SILVERBELL
*Halesia diptera* Ell.

A shrub or small tree with deciduous leaves, very finely toothed along the edges. Flowers are borne in clusters, usually three to five, with four waxy white petals and numerous stamens fused in a tight cluster. Widely distributed in rich woods, and on river bottoms and stream banks. February to March.

## Theaceae: Tea Family

Plate 111
LOBLOLLY BAY
*Gordonia lasianthus* (L.) Ell.

An evergreen tree native in warm climates; rare, but occasionally found in the southern part of the state. Leaves are alternate, slightly serrate, and usually clustered near the ends of branches, where fragrant white blossoms grow on stalks nearly as long as the leaves. Numerous orange stamens unite into a ring fused with the petals. The bark of mature trees is gray and deeply furrowed. In moist forests and low woods. June through August.

## Verbenaceae: Vervain Family

Plate 112
FRENCH MULBERRY, BEAUTY-BERRY
*Callicarpa americana* L.

A sprawling, ungainly shrub growing as high as six feet, beauty-berry was evidently named for its distinctive fruit rather than its inconspicuous pinkish flowers. *Callicarpa* is derived from the Greek for "beauty" and "fruit"; indeed, the royal purple berries are attractive, and sought by both birds and animals for food. Widely distributed in cutover woods and along streams. Fruits, September to November.

## Violaceae: Violet Family

Plate 113
BIRDS-FOOT VIOLET
*Viola pedata* L.

The largest of the many species of violets found in this area. It is classed as "stemless" since flowers and leaves grow individually from an underground stem. Leaves are divided into many narrow segments. Flowers are variable in color, from violet to purple to a rare pink. Petals are beardless, and a spot of white on the lower petal has a conspicuous stamen appendage of bright orange. In dry or sandy soil, sunny sites. March to April.

Plate 114
LITTLE WHITE VIOLET
*Viola primulifolia* L.

A fragrant little white violet found all over the Deep South. The soft leaves have somewhat winged and reddish stems. The lower lip of the flower is marked with tiny dark veins. Common in wet sites, along ditches and streams. March to May.

Plate 115
CONFEDERATE VIOLET
*Viola priceana* Pollard

Glossy green leaves from a stout underground stem form a striking contrast to the white or palest lavender flowers. The three lower petals are spotted with violet blue; all are heavily veined. Lateral petals have tufts of tiny white hairs; the lower petal is beardless. In woods and fields, and along roadsides. February to April.

## Vitaceae: Grape Family

Plate 116
SUMMER GRAPE
*Vitis aestivalis* Michaux

A high-climbing deciduous vine with serrate, shallowly or deeply lobed leaves, and intermittent, branched tendrils. The heavy drooping clusters of dark purple berries are enjoyed by birds. In low woods, and along damp roadsides and stream banks. September to October.

Plate 117
MUSCADINE
*Vitis rotundifolia* Michaux

Probably the best-known of the southern wild grapes, the ancestor of our cultivated scuppernong. A high-climbing, few-fruited vine with conspicuous tendrils, its young branches angled. Common in dryish, open, and disturbed woods. August to October.

# Index

Aceraceae, Plate 1
*Acer rubrum*, Plate 1
*Aesculus pavia*, Plate 61
*Agalinis purpurea*, Plate 108
Ageratum, wild, Plate 25
Alismataceae, Plate 2
Alternate leaf dogwood, Plate 41
Amaryllidaceae, Plates 3–4
Amaryllis family, Plates 3–4
American holly, Plate 7
*Amsonia tabernaemontana*, Plate 6
Anacardiaceae, Plate 5
*Anisostichus capreolata*, Plate 31
Apocynaceae, Plate 6
Aquifoliaceae, Plates 7–8
Araceae, Plates 9–10
*Arisaema triphyllum*, Plate 10
Aristolochiaceae, Plate 11
Arrowhead, Plate 2
Arum family, Plates 9–10
Asclepiadaceae, Plates 12–13
*Asclepias tuberosa*, Plate 12
*Asclepias variegata*, Plate 13
Aster, southern, Plate 14
Aster, stokes, Plate 15
Asteraceae, Plates 14–30
Aster family, Plates 14–30
*Aster hemisphericus*, Plate 14
Atamasco lily, Plate 3
Azalea, clammy, Plate 46
Azalea, orange-flowered, Plate 47
Azalea, summer, Plate 48
Azalea, swamp, Plate 48
Azalea, wild, Plate 49

Bachelor's button, Plate 93
Basil, red, Plate 67
Bay, loblolly, Plate 111
Bay, swamp, Plate 78
Bay, sweet, Plate 78
Beach morning-glory, Plate 38
Beauty-berry, Plate 112
Big-leaf magnolia, Plate 75
Bignoniaceae, Plates 31–32
Bignonia family, Plates 31–32
Birds-foot violet, Plate 113
Birthwort family, Plate 11
Bitter-weed, Plate 16
Black-eyed susan, Plate 17
Black locust, Plate 55
Bladderwort family, Plate 69
Blanket-flower, Plate 18

Bloodroot, Plate 89
Blue-star, Plate 6
Bog orchid, Plate 85
Bog torch, Plate 9
Buckeye, red, Plate 61
Buckeye family, Plate 61
Bull bay, Plate 77
Buttercup, Plate 84
Buttercup, early, Plate 94
Butterfly-weed, Plate 12
Butterwort, yellow, Plate 69

*Callicarpa americana*, Plate 112
*Callirhoë papaver*, Plate 81
*Calopogon pulchellus*, Plate 85
Calycanthaceae, Plate 33
Calycanthus family, Plate 33
*Calycanthus floridus*, Plate 33
*Campsis radicans*, Plate 32
Candy-root, low, Plate 93
Candy-root, orange, Plate 93
Caprifoliaceae, Plate 34
Carolina phlox, Plate 92
Carolina rose, Plate 99
Caryophyllaceae, Plate 35
*Cassia fasciculata*, Plate 57
Celastraceae, Plate 36
*Cercis canadensis*, Plate 58
Cherokee bean, Plate 53
*Cirsium virginianum*, Plate 29
Clammy azalea, Plate 46
*Cleistes divaricata*, Plate 87
Clematis, Plate 95
*Clematis crispa*, Plate 95
*Clematis viorna*, Plate 95
Commelinaceae, Plate 37
Coneflower, purple, Plate 19
Confederate violet, Plate 115
Convolvulaceae, Plates 38–40
Copper-colored iris, Plate 64
Coral honeysuckle, Plate 34
*Coreopsis major*, Plate 30
Cornaceae, Plates 41–43
*Cornus alternifolia*, Plate 41
*Cornus florida*, Plates 42–43
Cowcumber, Plate 75
Crab-apple, southern, Plate 96
Crab-apple, wild, Plate 96
*Crataegus marshallii*, Plate 97
*Crataegus opaca*, Plate 98
Crested dwarf iris, Plate 63
Crimson-eyed mallow, Plate 80

Crimson pitcher-plant, Plate 103
Cross vine, Plate 31
Crowfoot family, Plates 94–95
Crow poison, Plate 70
Cucumber tree, Plate 76
Cyperaceae, Plate 44

Daisy fleabane, Plate 20
Dayflower family, Plate 37
Dewberry, southern, Plates 100–101
*Dichromena colorata*, Plate 44
*Diospyros virginiana*, Plate 45
Dogbane family, Plate 6
Dogwood, alternate leaf, Plate 41
Dogwood, flowering (fall), Plate 43
Dogwood, flowering (spring), Plate 42
Dogwood family, Plates 41–43
Duck potato, Plate 2
Dune morning-glory, Plate 38

Early buttercup, Plate 94
Ebenaceae, Plate 45
Ebony family, Plate 45
*Echinacea purpurea*, Plate 19
Ericaceae, Plates 46–51
*Erigeron pulchellus*, Plate 20
*Erythrina herbacea*, Plate 53
*Euonymus americanus*, Plate 36
*Eupatorium coelestinum*, Plate 25
*Eupatorium purpureum*, Plate 24
Euphorbiaceae, Plate 52
*Euphorbia heterophylla*, Plate 52
Evening-primrose family, Plate 84

Fabaceae, Plates 53–58
Fetterbush, Plate 50
Figwort family, Plate 108
Fire pink, Plate 35
Flat-topped goldenrod, Plate 22
Flowering dogwood (fall), Plate 43
Flowering dogwood (spring), Plate 42
French mulberry, Plate 112
Fringed-orchid, white, Plate 86

Gaillardia, Plate 18
*Gaillardia aestivalis*, Plate 18
*Gelsemium sempervirens*, Plate 74
Gentianaceae, Plate 59
Gentian family, Plate 59

## 28 INDEX

Gerardia, purple, Plate 108
Ginger, wild, Plate 11
Goat's rue, Plate 54
Golden club, Plate 9
Goldenrod, Plate 21
Goldenrod, flat-topped, Plate 22
*Gordonia lasianthus*, Plate 111
Grape, summer, Plate 116
Grape family, Plates 116–17
Grass pink, Plate 85
Ground cherry, Plate 109

*Habenaria blephariglottis*, Plate 86
*Halesia diptera*, Plate 110
Hamamelidaceae, Plate 60
Hawthorn, parsley, Plate 97
Heart leaf, Plate 11
Hearts a-bustin' with love, Plate 36
Heath family, Plates 46–51
*Helenium amarum*, Plate 16
*Helenium autumnale*, Plate 26
*Helianthus angustifolius*, Plate 28
*Helianthus tuberosus*, Plate 23
*Hexastylis arifolia*, Plate 11
Hibiscus, pineland, Plate 80
*Hibiscus moscheutos*, Plate 80
Hippocastanaceae, Plate 61
Holly, American, Plate 7
Holly family, Plates 7–8
Honeysuckle, coral, Plate 34
Honeysuckle, pink, Plate 49
Honeysuckle, swamp, Plate 46
Honeysuckle, trumpet, Plate 34
Honeysuckle family, Plate 34
Horsemint, Plate 68
Hydrangea, oak-leaf, Plates 106–7
*Hydrangea quercifolia*, Plates 106–7
*Hymenocallis occidentalis*, Plate 4

*Ilex opaca*, Plate 7
*Ilex vomitoria*, Plate 8
Illiciaceae, Plate 62
Illicium family, Plate 62
*Illicium floridanum*, Plate 62
Indian pink, Plate 73
*Ipomoea pandurata*, Plate 40
*Ipomoea stolonifera*, Plate 38
*Ipomoea trichocarpa*, Plate 39
Iridaceae, Plates 63–66
Iris, copper-colored, Plate 64
Iris, crested dwarf, Plate 63
Iris, red, Plate 64
Iris, zig-zag-stemmed, Plate 66
*Iris brevicaulis*, Plate 66
*Iris cristata*, Plate 63
Iris family, Plates 63–66
*Iris fulva*, Plate 64
*Iris virginica*, Plate 65

Jack-in-the-pulpit, Plate 10
Jerusalem artichoke, Plate 23
Jessamine, yellow, Plate 74
Joe-pye weed, Plate 24

*Kalmia latifolia*, Plate 51

Lady lupine, Plate 56
Lamiaceae, Plates 67–68
Leather-flower, Plate 95
Legume family, Plates 53–58
Lentibulariaceae, Plate 69
Leopard lily, Plate 71
*Leucothoe axillaris*, Plate 50
Liliaceae, Plates 70–72
*Lilium catesbaei*, Plate 71
Lily, atamasco, Plate 3
Lily, southern pine, Plate 71
Lily family, Plates 70–72
*Liquidambar styraciflua*, Plate 60
*Liriodendron tulipifera*, Plate 79
Little sweet betsy, Plate 72
Little white violet, Plate 114
Loblolly bay, Plate 111
Locust, black, Plate 55
Loganiaceae, Plates 73–74
Logania family, Plates 73–74
*Lonicera sempervirens*, Plate 34
Low candy-root, Plate 93
*Lupinus villosus*, Plate 56

Madder family, Plate 102
Magnolia, big-leaf, Plate 75
Magnolia, southern, Plate 77
*Magnolia acuminata*, Plate 76
Magnoliaceae, Plates 75–79
Magnolia family, Plates 75–79
*Magnolia grandiflora*, Plate 77
*Magnolia macrophylla*, Plate 75
*Magnolia virginiana*, Plate 78
Mallow, crimson-eyed, Plate 80
Mallow family, Plates 80–81
*Malus angustifolia*, Plate 96
Malvaceae, Plates 80–81
Mamou, Plate 53
Man of earth, Plate 40
Maple, red, Plate 1
Maple, swamp, Plate 1
Maple family, Plate 1
Mayhaw, Plate 98
Maypop, Plate 90
Meadow beauty, Plate 82
Melastoma family, Plate 82
Melastomataceae, Plate 82
Milkweed, orange, Plate 12
Milkweed, white, Plate 13
Milkweed family, Plates 12–13
Milkwort family, Plate 93
Mint family, Plates 67–68

Mistflower, Plate 25
*Mitchella repens*, Plate 102
*Monarda punctata*, Plate 68
Morning-glory, beach, Plate 38
Morning-glory, dune, Plate 38
Morning-glory, wild, Plate 39
Morning-glory family, Plates 38–40
Mountain laurel, Plate 51
Mulberry, french, Plate 112
Muscadine, Plate 117

Narrow-leaved sunflower, Plate 28
Nightshade family, Plate 109
Nymphaeaceae, Plate 83
*Nymphaea odorata*, Plate 83

Oak-leaf hydrangea, Plates 106–7
*Oenothera speciosa*, Plate 84
Onagraceae, Plate 84
Orange candy-root, Plate 93
Orange-flowered azalea, Plate 47
Orange milkweed, Plate 12
Orchid, bog, Plate 85
Orchid, rosebud, Plate 87
Orchidaceae, Plates 85–87
Orchid family, Plates 85–87
*Orontium aquaticum*, Plate 9
Oxalidaceae, Plate 88
*Oxalis*, Plate 88

Painted-leaf, Plate 52
Papaveraceae, Plate 89
Parrot pitcher-plant, Plate 104
Parsley hawthorn, Plate 97
Partridge berry, Plate 102
Partridge pea, Plate 57
Passifloraceae, Plates 90–91
*Passiflora incarnata*, Plate 90
*Passiflora lutea*, Plate 91
Passion-flower, Plate 90
Passion-flower, yellow, Plate 91
Passion-flower family, Plates 90–91
Persimmon, Plate 45
Phlox, carolina, Plate 92
*Phlox carolina*, Plate 92
Phlox family, Plate 92
*Physalis angulata*, Plate 109
Pineland ginseng, Plate 27
Pineland hibiscus, Plate 80
*Pinguicula lutea*, Plate 69
Pink family, Plate 35
Pink honeysuckle, Plate 49
Pitcher-plant, crimson, Plate 103
Pitcher-plant, parrot, Plate 104
Pitcher-plant, yellow, Plate 105
Pitcher-plant family, Plates 103–5
Pogonia, rose, Plate 85
Pogonia, spreading, Plate 87

# INDEX

*Pogonia ophioglossoides*, Plate 85
Poinsettia, wild, Plate 52
Polemoniaceae, Plate 92
Polygalaceae, Plate 93
*Polygala lutea*, Plate 93
*Polygala nana*, Plate 93
Poplar, yellow, Plate 79
Poppy family, Plate 89
Poppy-mallow, Plate 81
Primrose, Plate 84
Purple coneflower, Plate 19
Purple gerardia, Plate 108
Purple thistle, Plate 29
Purple trillium, Plate 72

Ranunculaceae, Plates 94–95
*Ranunculus fascicularis*, Plate 94
Red basil, Plate 67
Red buckeye, Plate 61
Redbud, Plate 58
Red iris, Plate 64
Red maple, Plate 1
*Rhexia alifanus*, Plate 82
*Rhododendron austrinum*, Plate 47
*Rhododendron canescens*, Plate 49
*Rhododendron serrulatum*, Plate 48
*Rhododendron viscosum*, Plate 46
*Rhus copallina*, Plate 5
*Robinia pseudo-acacia*, Plate 55
Robin's-plantain, Plate 20
*Rosa carolina*, Plate 99
Rosaceae, Plates 96–101
Rose, carolina, Plate 99
Rose, wild, Plate 99
Rosebud orchid, Plate 87
Rose family, Plates 96–101
Rose-gentian, Plate 59
Rose pogonia, Plate 85
Rubiaceae, Plate 102
*Rubus trivialis*, Plates 100–101
*Rudbeckia hirta*, Plate 17

*Sabatia brachiata*, Plate 59
*Sagittaria lancifolia*, Plate 2
*Sanguinaria canadensis*, Plate 89
Sarraceniaceae, Plates 103–5
*Sarracenia drummondii*, Plate 103
*Sarracenia flava*, Plate 105
*Sarracenia psittacina*, Plate 104
*Satureja coccineum*, Plate 67
Saxifragaceae, Plates 106–7
Saxifrage family, Plates 106–7
Scrophulariaceae, Plate 108
Sedge, white-topped, Plate 44
Sedge family, Plate 44

*Silene virginica*, Plate 35
Silverbell, Plate 110
Slim pod, Plate 6
Sneezeweed, Plate 26
Solanaceae, Plate 109
*Solidago pinetorum*, Plate 21
*Solidago tenuifolia*, Plate 22
Southern aster, Plate 14
Southern blue flag, Plate 65
Southern crab-apple, Plate 96
Southern dewberry (flower), Plate 100
Southern dewberry (fruit), Plate 101
Southern magnolia, Plate 77
Southern pine lily, Plate 71
Spider-lily, Plate 4
Spiderwort, Plate 37
*Spigelia marilandica*, Plate 73
Spreading pogonia, Plate 87
Spurge family, Plate 52
Staff-tree family, Plate 36
Star-anise, Plate 62
Star-bush, Plate 62
Stokes aster, Plate 15
Stokesia, Plate 15
*Stokesia laevis*, Plate 15
Storax family, Plate 110
Strawberry bush, Plate 36
Styracaceae, Plate 110
Sumac, wing-rib, Plate 5
Sumac family, Plate 5
Summer azalea, Plate 48
Summer grape, Plate 116
Sunflower, Plate 27
Sunflower, narrow-leaved, Plate 28
Sunflower family, Plates 14–30
Swamp azalea, Plate 48
Swamp bay, Plate 78
Swamp honeysuckle, Plate 46
Swamp maple, Plate 1
Sweet bay, Plate 78
Sweet-gum, Plate 60
Sweet shrub, Plate 33

Tea family, Plate 111
*Tephrosia virginiana*, Plate 54
*Tetragonotheca helianthoides*, Plate 27
Theaceae, Plate 111
Thistle, purple, Plate 29
*Tradescantia*, Plate 37
Trillium, purple, Plate 72
*Trillium cuneatum*, Plate 72
Trumpet-creeper, Plate 32

Trumpet honeysuckle, Plate 34
Trumpet vine, Plate 32
Tulip tree, Plate 79

Umbrella tree, Plate 75

Verbenaceae, Plate 112
Vervain family, Plate 112
Violaceae, Plates 113–15
*Viola pedata*, Plate 113
*Viola priceana*, Plate 115
*Viola primulifolia*, Plate 114
Violet, birds-foot, Plate 113
Violet, confederate, Plate 115
Violet, little white, Plate 114
Violet family, Plates 113–15
Violet wood sorrel, Plate 88
Vitaceae, Plates 116–17
*Vitis aestivalis*, Plate 116
*Vitis rotundifolia*, Plate 117

Water-lily, white, Plate 83
Water-lily family, Plate 83
Water-plantain family, Plate 2
White fringed-orchid, Plate 86
White milkweed, Plate 13
White-topped sedge, Plate 44
White water-lily, Plate 83
Whorled tickseed, Plate 30
Wild ageratum, Plate 25
Wild azalea, Plate 49
Wild crab-apple, Plate 96
Wild ginger, Plate 11
Wild morning-glory, Plate 39
Wild poinsettia, Plate 52
Wild-potato, Plate 40
Wild rose, Plate 99
Windflower, Plate 84
Wine cup, Plate 81
Wing-rib sumac, Plate 5
Witch-hazel family, Plate 60
Wood-sorrel family, Plate 88

Yaupon, Plate 8
Yellow butterwort, Plate 69
Yellow jessamine, Plate 74
Yellow passion-flower, Plate 91
Yellow pitcher-plant, Plate 105
Yellow poplar, Plate 79

*Zephyranthes atamasco*, Plate 3
*Zigadenus angustifolia*, Plate 70
Zig-zag-stemmed iris, Plate 66

# Bibliography

Bailey, L. H. *Manual of Cultivated Plants*. rev. ed. New York: MacMillan Company, 1971.

Brown, Clair H. *Wildflowers of Louisiana*. Baton Rouge: Louisiana State University Press, 1972.

Collingwood, C. H., and Brush, Warren D. *Knowing Your Trees*. 2d rev. ed. Washington: American Forestry Association, 1964.

Dean, Blanche E.; Mason, Amy; and Thomas, Joab L. *Wildflowers of Alabama and Adjoining States*. Tuscaloosa: University of Alabama Press, 1973.

Dorman, Caroline. *Flowers Native to the South*. 2d ed. Chapel Hill: University of North Carolina Press, 1959.

Greene, Wilhelmina F., and Blomquist, Hugo L. *Flowers of the South*. Chapel Hill: University of North Carolina Press, 1953.

Niering, William A. *The Audubon Society Field Guide to North American Wild Flowers, Eastern Region*. New York: Alfred A. Knopf, 1979.

Radford, A. E.; Ahles, H. E.; and Bell, C. R. *Manual of the Vascular Flora of the Carolinas*. rev. ed. Chapel Hill: University of North Carolina Press, 1968.

Rickett, Harold William. *Wildflowers of the United States*, vol. II, *The Southeastern States*. New York: McGraw-Hill, 1968.

Rogers, Ken E. "Annotated List of the Vascular Flora of Covington, Forrest, Jones, Lamar and Perry Counties, Mississippi," based upon field studies made by the author during the period 1969 through 1974 while on the faculty of the University of Southern Mississippi. Unpublished.

# MISSISSIPPI WILDFLOWERS

Plate 1
RED MAPLE, SWAMP MAPLE
*Acer rubrum* L.

Plate 2
DUCK POTATO, ARROWHEAD
*Sagittaria lancifolia* L.

Plate 3
ATAMASCO LILY
*Zephyranthes atamasco* (L.) Herbert

Plate 4
SPIDER-LILY
*Hymenocallis occidentalis* (Le-Conte) Kunth

Plate 5
WING-RIB SUMAC
*Rhus copallina* L.

Plate 6
BLUE-STAR, SLIM POD
*Amsonia tabernaemontana* Walter

Plate 7
AMERICAN HOLLY
*Ilex opaca* Aiton

Plate 8
YAUPON
*Ilex vomitoria* Aiton

Plate 9
GOLDEN CLUB, BOG TORCH
*Orontium aquaticum* L.

Plate 10
JACK-IN-THE-PULPIT
*Arisaema triphyllum* (L.) Schott

Plate 11
HEART LEAF, WILD GINGER
*Hexastylis arifolia* (Michaux) Small

Plate 12
BUTTERFLY-WEED,
ORANGE MILKWEED
*Asclepias tuberosa* L.

Plate 13
WHITE MILKWEED
*Asclepias variegata* L.

Plate 14
SOUTHERN ASTER
*Aster hemisphericus* (Alex.) Shinners

Plate 15
STOKES ASTER, STOKESIA
*Stokesia laevis* (Hill) Greene

Plate 16
BITTER-WEED
*Helenium amarum* (Raf.) H. Rock

Plate 17
BLACK-EYED SUSAN
*Rudbeckia hirta* L.

Plate 18
BLANKET-FLOWER, GAILLARDIA
*Gaillardia aestivalis* (Walter) H. Rock

Plate 19
PURPLE CONEFLOWER
*Echinacea purpurea* (L.) Moench

Plate 20
DAISY FLEABANE, ROBIN'S-PLANTAIN
*Erigeron pulchellus* Michaux

Plate 21
GOLDENROD
*Solidago pinetorum* Small

Plate 22
FLAT-TOPPED GOLDENROD
*Solidago tenuifolia* Pursh.

Plate 23
JERUSALEM ARTICHOKE
*Helianthus tuberosus* L.

Plate 24
JOE-PYE WEED
*Eupatorium purpureum* L.

Plate 25
MISTFLOWER, WILD AGERATUM
*Eupatorium coelestinum* L.

Plate 26
SNEEZEWEED
*Helenium autumnale* L.

Plate 27
SUNFLOWER, PINELAND GINSENG
*Tetragonotheca helianthoides* L.

Plate 28
NARROW-LEAVED SUNFLOWER
*Helianthus angustifolius* L.

Plate 29
PURPLE THISTLE
*Cirsium virginianum* L.

Plate 30
WHORLED TICKSEED
*Coreopsis major* Walter

Plate 31
CROSS VINE
*Anisostichus capreolata* (L.) Bureau

Plate 32
TRUMPET-CREEPER, TRUMPET VINE
*Campsis radicans* (L.) Seemann

Plate 33
SWEET SHRUB
*Calycanthus floridus* L.

Plate 34
CORAL HONEYSUCKLE,
TRUMPET HONEYSUCKLE
*Lonicera sempervirens* L.

Plate 35
FIRE PINK
*Silene virginica* L.

Plate 36
HEARTS A-BUSTIN' WITH LOVE,
STRAWBERRY BUSH
*Euonymus americanus* L.

Plate 37
SPIDERWORT
*Tradescantia* spp.

Plate 38
DUNE MORNING-GLORY,
BEACH MORNING-GLORY
*Ipomoea stolonifera* (Cyrillo) Poir.

Plate 39
WILD MORNING-GLORY
*Ipomoea trichocarpa* Ell.

Plate 40
WILD-POTATO, MAN OF EARTH
*Ipomoea pandurata* (L.) Meyer

Plate 41
ALTERNATE LEAF DOGWOOD
*Cornus alternifolia* L.f.

Plate 42
FLOWERING DOGWOOD (Spring)
*Cornus florida* L.

Plate 43
FLOWERING DOGWOOD (Fall)
*Cornus florida* L.

Plate 44
**WHITE-TOPPED SEDGE**
*Dichromena colorata* (L.) Hitchcock

Plate 45
PERSIMMON
*Diospyros virginiana* L.

Plate 46
CLAMMY AZALEA,
SWAMP HONEYSUCKLE
*Rhododendron viscosum* (L.) Torrey

Plate 47
ORANGE-FLOWERED AZALEA
*Rhododendron austrinum* (Small) Mill.

Plate 48
SUMMER AZALEA, SWAMP AZALEA
*Rhododendron serrulatum* (Small) Mill.

Plate 49
WILD AZALEA, PINK HONEYSUCKLE
*Rhododendron canescens* (Michaux) Sweet

Plate 50
FETTERBUSH
*Leucothoe axillaris* (Lam.) D. Don

Plate 51
MOUNTAIN LAUREL
*Kalmia latifolia* L.

Plate 52
WILD POINSETTIA, PAINTED-LEAF
*Euphorbia heterophylla* L.

Plate 53
**CHEROKEE BEAN, MAMOU**
*Erythrina herbacea* L.

Plate 54
GOAT'S RUE
*Tephrosia virginiana* (L.) Persoon

Plate 55
BLACK LOCUST
*Robinia pseudo-acacia* L.

Plate 56
LADY LUPINE
*Lupinus villosus* Willd.

Plate 57
PARTRIDGE PEA
*Cassia fasciculata* Michaux

Plate 58
REDBUD
*Cercis canadensis* L.

Plate 59
ROSE-GENTIAN
*Sabatia brachiata* Ell.

Plate 60
SWEET-GUM
*Liquidambar styraciflua* L.

Plate 61
RED BUCKEYE
*Aesculus pavia* L.

Plate 62
STAR-ANISE, STAR-BUSH
*Illicium floridanum* Ell.

Plate 63
CRESTED DWARF IRIS
*Iris cristata* Aiton

Plate 64
RED IRIS, COPPER-COLORED IRIS
*Iris fulva* Ker

Plate 65
SOUTHERN BLUE FLAG
*Iris virginica* L.

Plate 66
ZIG-ZAG-STEMMED IRIS
*Iris brevicaulis* Raf.

Plate 67
RED BASIL
*Satureja coccineum* (Nutt.) Kuntze

Plate 68
HORSEMINT
*Monarda punctata* L.

Plate 69
YELLOW BUTTERWORT
*Pinguicula lutea* Walter

Plate 70
CROW POISON
*Zigadenus angustifolia* (Michaux) Swats

Plate 71
SOUTHERN PINE LILY, LEOPARD LILY
*Lilium catesbaei* Walter

Plate 72
PURPLE TRILLIUM,
LITTLE SWEET BETSY
*Trillium cuneatum* Raf.

Plate 73
INDIAN PINK
*Spigelia marilandica* L.

Plate 74
YELLOW JESSAMINE
*Gelsemium sempervirens* (L.) Aiton f.

Plate 75
COWCUMBER, UMBRELLA TREE,
BIG-LEAF MAGNOLIA
*Magnolia macrophylla* Michaux

Plate 76
CUCUMBER TREE
*Magnolia acuminata* L.

Plate 77
SOUTHERN MAGNOLIA, BULL BAY
*Magnolia grandiflora* L.

Plate 78
SWEET BAY, SWAMP BAY
*Magnolia virginiana* L.

Plate 79
TULIP TREE, YELLOW POPLAR
*Liriodendron tulipifera* L.

Plate 80
CRIMSON-EYED MALLOW,
PINELAND HIBISCUS
*Hibiscus moscheutos* L.

Plate 81
POPPY-MALLOW, WINE CUP
*Callirhoë papaver* (Cav.) Gray

Plate 82
MEADOW BEAUTY
*Rhexia alifanus* Walter

Plate 83
WHITE WATER-LILY
*Nymphaea odorata* Aiton

Plate 84
PRIMROSE, BUTTERCUP,
WINDFLOWER
*Oenothera speciosa* Nutt.

Plate 85
BOG ORCHID, GRASS PINK
*Calopogon pulchellus* R. Br.
ROSE POGONIA
*Pogonia ophioglossoides* (L.) Ker

Plate 86
WHITE FRINGED-ORCHID
*Habenaria blephariglottis* (Willd.) Hooker

Plate 87
ROSEBUD ORCHID,
SPREADING POGONIA
*Cleistes divaricata* (L.) Ames

Plate 88
VIOLET WOOD SORREL
*Oxalis* spp.

Plate 89
BLOODROOT
*Sanguinaria canadensis* L.

Plate 90
MAYPOP, PASSION-FLOWER
*Passiflora incarnata* L.

Plate 91
YELLOW PASSION-FLOWER
*Passiflora lutea* L.

Plate 92
CAROLINA PHLOX
*Phlox carolina* L.

Plate 93
ORANGE CANDY-ROOT
*Polygala lutea* L.

LOW CANDY-ROOT,
BACHELOR'S BUTTON
*Polygala nana* (Michaux) DC.

Plate 94
EARLY BUTTERCUP
*Ranunculus fascicularis* Muhl.

Plate 95
LEATHER-FLOWER, CLEMATIS
*Clematis crispa* L.

Plate 96
WILD CRAB-APPLE,
SOUTHERN CRAB-APPLE
*Malus angustifolia* (Aiton) Michaux

Plate 97
PARSLEY HAWTHORN
*Crataegus marshallii* Eggl.

Plate 98
MAYHAW
*Crataegus opaca* Hooker and Arn.

Plate 99
CAROLINA ROSE, WILD ROSE
*Rosa carolina* L.

Plate 100
SOUTHERN DEWBERRY (Flower)
*Rubus trivialis* Michaux

Plate 101
SOUTHERN DEWBERRY (Fruit)
*Rubus trivialis* Michaux

Plate 102
PARTRIDGE BERRY
*Mitchella repens* L.

Plate 103
CRIMSON PITCHER-PLANT
*Sarracenia drummondii* Croom

Plate 104
PARROT PITCHER-PLANT
*Sarracenia psittacina* Michaux

Plate 105
YELLOW PITCHER-PLANT
*Sarracenia flava* L.

Plate 106
OAK-LEAF HYDRANGEA
*Hydrangea quercifolia* Bartr.

Plate 107
OAK-LEAF HYDRANGEA
*Hydrangea quercifolia* Bartr.

Plate 108
PURPLE GERARDIA
*Agalinis purpurea* (L.) Pennell

Plate 109
GROUND CHERRY
*Physalis angulata* L.

Plate 110
SILVERBELL
*Halesia diptera* Ell.

Plate 111
LOBLOLLY BAY
*Gordonia lasianthus* (L.) Ell.

Plate 112
FRENCH MULBERRY, BEAUTY-BERRY
*Callicarpa americana* L.

Plate 113
BIRDS-FOOT VIOLET
*Viola pedata* L.

Plate 114
LITTLE WHITE VIOLET
*Viola primulifolia* L.

Plate 115
CONFEDERATE VIOLET
*Viola priceana* Pollard

Plate 116
SUMMER GRAPE
*Vitis aestivalis* Michaux

Plate 117
MUSCADINE
*Vitis rotundifolia* Michaux